Contents

Chapter	1	The man without a name	5
Chapter	2	Nurse Angela	9
Chapter	3	Who is John Roberts?	14
Chapter	4	Waiting	20
Chapter	5	Goodbye, holiday	24
Chapter	6	A cup of coffee	28

People in the story

Doctor Cox
Nurse Angela
Detective Jenny Brown
Susan Peters, a television producer
John Doe

Places in the story

King Alfred's Winchester

Martial Rose Library
Tel: 01962 827306

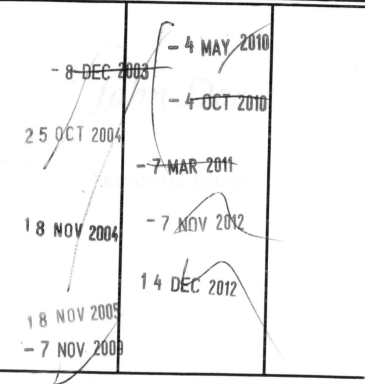

- 8 DEC 2003

25 OCT 2004

1 8 NOV 2004

1 8 NOV 2005

- 7 NOV 2005

- 4 MAY 2010

- 4 OCT 2010

- 7 MAR 2011

- 7 NOV 2012

1 4 DEC 2012

To be returned on or before the day marked above, subject to recall.

PUBLISHED BY THE PRESS SYNDICATE OF THE UNIVERSITY OF CAMBRIDGE
The Pitt Building, Trumpington Street, Cambridge CB2 1RP, United Kingdom

CAMBRIDGE UNIVERSITY PRESS
The Edinburgh Building, Cambridge CB2 2RU, United Kingdom
40 West 20th Street, New York, NY 10011-4211, USA
10 Stamford Road, Oakleigh, Melbourne 3166, Australia

Printed in the United Kingdom at the University Press, Cambridge

Typeset in 12/15pt Adobe Garamond [CE]

ISBN 0 521 65619 2

Chapter 1 *The man without a name*

'What's your name?' asked Doctor Cox.

The man in the bed did not answer.

'Open your eyes,' said Doctor Cox.

The man in the bed opened his eyes. He looked at the doctor.

'Do you understand the question?' asked Doctor Cox.

'Yes,' said the man in the bed. 'I do.'

'Good,' said Doctor Cox again. The doctor smiled at the man. It was a nice smile. 'And do you know your name?'

'No,' said the man in the bed. 'I don't know what my name is.'

The man in the bed said nothing for a moment. The doctor waited and watched him.

'Who is this man?' thought Doctor Cox. 'I don't know who he is or where he comes from. I know that a woman found him yesterday in the street. The woman telephoned the police and the police brought him here to the hospital. I know he had blue jeans and a jacket, a green shirt and black socks and shoes. His clothes were clean, but he had no money and no papers.'

'I'm Doctor Philip Cox,' Doctor Cox said to the man. 'You can call me Philip.'

'You're a doctor,' said the man. He looked at the doctor. 'And this is a hospital.' The man in the bed spoke very slowly.

'Yes,' answered Doctor Cox, but now he did not smile. 'What's the problem with this man?' thought Doctor Cox. 'He has language. He understands words, but he doesn't know who he is or where he comes from. Does he remember or doesn't he?' The police don't know who he is. I don't know who he is. And we need to know these things. Somewhere, somebody is waiting for him.

'You look at a man and what do you see?' thought Doctor Cox. 'You see very little. It's not easy to know a man without language. You need words, you need names and places. People have family and friends. Who am I, for example?' he thought.

'I'm a doctor. Yes, this is my work. At the hospital I'm Doctor Cox. But my friends and my wife know me as Philip and my children know me as Dad. They don't know

Doctor Cox. Doctor Cox, Philip and Dad. They are all me, but they are not the same. Without family and friends, and without work, what am I? I need to know more, much more, about this man,' he thought. He spoke to the man again.

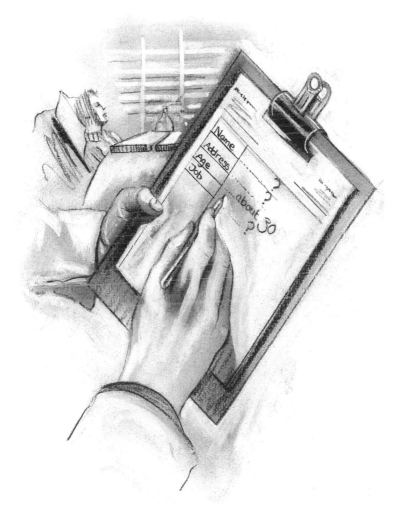

'We're going to find out who you are,' said Doctor Cox. He sat on the man's bed and smiled at him. 'You must be somebody's husband or somebody's son or somebody's brother. Somewhere there are people looking for you, waiting for you. I want to help you. I need to find who you are and then I can help you.'

'Thank you, Doctor,' said the man in the bed.

'Where do you come from? Do you think you live near here?' asked Doctor Cox.

'Where is here?' the man in the bed asked him.

'Here?' answered Doctor Cox. 'This is Exeter. We are in Exeter, in Devon, in England.'

'I don't know where I come from,' said the man. 'I don't think it's Exeter. I don't think I know Exeter.'

'When we find a man and we don't know his name,' said Doctor Cox, 'we call him John Doe. Can I call you John?'

'I saw a man in a film called John Doe,' said the man in the bed. He looked at the doctor and smiled.

'That's good,' said Doctor Cox. 'That's very good. You remember that. You went to a film. What was the film?'

'I don't know, Doctor. I don't remember very much. I remember I went to the film. It was in a big cinema. There was a man called John Doe in the film, but I think he was dead.'

'You're not dead, John,' said the Doctor. 'You're alive. But I want to know who you are. I need to know who you are. I need to ask you some questions.'

'OK, Doctor,' said John. 'Ask your questions.'

Chapter 2 *Nurse Angela*

There is a man near my bed. His clothes are white. No. Some of his clothes are white. He has a white coat, but his trousers are brown. He also has brown hair. The man in the white coat says he's a doctor. He says his name is Doctor Cox. He tells me to call him Philip. He says he is going to help me.

But he's not going to help me. They think I don't remember. They think I don't know anything. They know nothing, the doctors. Or the police. Nobody knows who I am. I sit in the bed and answer questions. They ask lots of questions.

'Do you know what amnesia is, John?' Doctor Cox asks me.

Doctor Cox. Doctor Philip Cox. He thinks he's somebody. He's nobody. I know what amnesia is.

'Yes,' I say. 'It's when you can't remember anything. You don't know who you are or where you come from. You don't know who your wife is or where your home is.'

'Do you have a wife?' Doctor Cox asks me. He's very quick, this doctor. I had a wife. But I don't tell him. I don't tell him anything. He calls me John Doe. That makes me smile. My name *is* John. I have lots of names, lots of surnames ... but my first name is always John. The doctor doesn't know that.

'Do you think I have amnesia?' I ask him.

'I want to find out, John,' says Doctor Cox. 'You tell me. Do you think you have amnesia?'

I ask a question. He answers with a question. I don't like that.

'I don't know, Philip. I'm very tired,' I say.

Doctor Cox looks at his watch.

'It's eleven o'clock now,' he says. 'I'm going on holiday tomorrow and I have lots of work to do. Today lots of people want to see me. I must go. But we can talk again this afternoon.'

'Thank you, Doctor,' I say.

'Don't be afraid, John,' says Doctor Cox. 'Everything's going to be all right very soon. I know these things. You're afraid that you're nobody, but I know that you're somebody.'

'I *am* somebody,' I say. Afraid! I'm not afraid. I'm not afraid of anybody or anything. But I don't say that. I say: 'I'm somebody, but I don't know who I am.' That's not true. I do know who I am. But I'm not telling him. I'm not telling anybody.

I watch Doctor Cox. He goes to the door.

'Nurse!' he calls. 'Can I talk to you for a minute, please?'

A nurse comes into the room. She is very beautiful. She smiles at the doctor. She smiles at me. Doctor Cox calls her Angela. Nurse Angela. I like that. I like the name Angela.

'Yes, doctor,' says Nurse Angela. She has short black hair and beautiful black eyes.

'Are you here all day today?' asks Doctor Cox.

'Yes, doctor,' answers Nurse Angela.

'Good. It's about this man in bed number six.' Doctor Cox is standing by the door and he speaks very quietly. He thinks I can't hear. But I can hear him.

The doctor talks to Nurse Angela about me.

'Ask him lots of questions,' he says. He wants me to remember.

He wants to know who I am. He wants me to say, 'I know who I am'. He's going to wait a long time for me to say that.

Nurse Angela sits by my bed. She smiles. She has a big, big smile.

'Hello, John,' she says to me. She has a beautiful, quiet voice. 'And how are we today?'

Why do nurses and doctors say 'we' when they mean 'you'? I don't like that. They say 'Are we hungry?' when they mean 'Are you hungry?' That's what you say to very small children. 'How are we then? Aren't we a big boy?' they say to babies. Babies can't answer, but I can. And I'm not a small child. I don't like you now, Nurse Angela. You're going to be sorry.

'Go away, nurse,' I say very quietly.

'What did you say?' asks Nurse Angela. 'I didn't hear what you said.'

'I said "hello",' I say. She's not going away. She wants a conversation. She wants to talk.

'My name is Angela,' she says. 'I come from Birmingham. But my family comes from London. Do you know Birmingham?'

'No,' I say. That's not true. I know Birmingham. I had a house in Birmingham. 'I don't think so. But ...' I stop. 'Is this Birmingham?' I know it's Exeter. The doctor told me it was Exeter, but she doesn't know that.

Nurse Angela smiles. It's a beautiful smile. I look at her. She is small, with a nice face. I smile at her. I knew another woman with a nice face. She lived in Birmingham. She wasn't nice to me. She died in Birmingham.

Angela talks. She says I must talk, too. She says she's going to say a word and I must answer with another word. I must say the first word I think of. She says it's going to help me remember.

'Night,' she says.

'Day,' I answer.

She says more words. I answer with more words.

'Afternoon,' she says.

'Morning,' I answer.

Book: paper. Father: mother. It's easy.

'Woman,' says Angela.

'Dead,' I answer.

'What?' asks Angela.

'Bed,' I say quickly. She writes something.

I didn't want to say that ... I spoke too quickly. Angela says another word. I answer. Window: door. Rain: sun. Water: sea. Why did I say dead? I think. I didn't want to say that. Bad boy, John, I say to myself. You're a bad boy.

Angela stops. 'You did very well,' she says. 'Are you hungry?' she asks.

'Yes,' I tell her. 'I'm very hungry.'

'Good,' she says. 'Would you like something to eat?'

'Yes, please, Angela,' I say. I smile.

'OK,' says Angela. 'Would you like some eggs and some bread?'

'Thank you,' I say. 'Yes.' I take her hand. I smile. 'Thank you, Nurse Angela.'

Chapter 3   *Who is John Roberts?*

Detective Jenny Brown walked along the street. It was a beautiful sunny day. There were lots of people in the street. Children ran down the street to school. People talked to each other and laughed.

Jenny loved the city of York. It was a beautiful place to live. But bad things can happen anywhere, she thought. Bad things can happen in beautiful places, too.

Jenny went into a building. It was a television studio. Jenny walked to the reception.

'Hello,' said Jenny to the receptionist. 'I'm Detective Jenny Brown. I'm here to see Susan Peters, the television producer. She makes the programme "Crimeseek".'

'Is that the programme where the police tell you about the crimes in York?' asked the receptionist.

'Yes,' said Jenny Brown, 'that's right.'

A few minutes later Susan Peters came down the stairs to the reception.

'Hello, Jenny,' Susan Peters said. 'Come to my office. We can talk there.' They went to Susan's office.

'Please, sit down,' said Susan. 'Would you like a coffee, Jenny?'

'No, thank you,' said Jenny. 'I'm fine.'

'I hope we can help you,' said Susan.

'We want your help about a woman who died. Did you read about it in the newspapers?'

TELEVISION STUDIOS

15

'Yes,' said Susan, 'but the newspapers don't say very much. Tell me about her. Tell me what happened.'

'I can tell you everything the police know,' Jenny told Susan. 'But we don't know very much. We need to know more. That's why we hope your programme "Crimeseek" can help us.'

'We'll do everything we can,' said Susan.

'On Saturday,' said Jenny, 'a woman came to see the police. She said she was very worried about her friend. Her friend's name was Mary. The woman played tennis with Mary every Saturday. But this Saturday she waited and waited and Mary didn't come.

'The woman was very unhappy. She phoned Mary's number lots and lots of times. But nobody answered. She wanted to go to Mary's house but she didn't want to go alone.

'She asked the police to go with her. I went to the house at three o'clock that afternoon,' said Jenny. 'There was no answer, but the door was open. I went in. A woman was on the floor. It was Mary. She was dead.'

'The newspaper said that Mary died on Friday night,' Susan said.

'Yes,' said Jenny. 'About eleven o'clock, we think.'

'What else did you find?' Susan asked Jenny.

'Well,' said Jenny, 'we think that Mary knew the person who killed her. We think that he or she came to dinner on Friday. There were two plates and two glasses in the kitchen. Then we talked to Mary's friends and to the people she worked with.' Jenny gave Susan a piece of paper.

Dear Mum,

I'm sorry I didn't write last week, but thank you for your letter. Now I have something important to tell you. I met a man! Not any man, I think, but THE MAN!!

His name is John Roberts and he is 29. He works in a restaurant now, but he wants to work in films. Anyway, I'm very happy and I know you're going to like him, too.

He's coming to dinner tonight. I'm making my famous chocolate cake. And I'm wearing my red dress. I must stop now and

'Then we found this,' Jenny said.

Susan looked at the paper.

'It's a letter Mary wrote on Friday,' said Jenny. 'But she didn't finish it.'

Read letter →

'Is that the end of the letter?' asked Susan.

'Yes,' answered Jenny.

'Who is John Roberts?' asked Susan.

'We don't know,' said Jenny. 'That's why I need your help. We need to find him. I know he came here, to York, in July. He worked at an Italian restaurant. They said he

18

was very quiet. They liked him. But he didn't go to work on Friday. After Friday nobody saw him. We can't find him anywhere.'

'Do you have a photograph of John Roberts?' asked Susan.

'Yes, here,' said Jenny. Jenny gave Susan the photograph.

Susan looked at it. It was of a man. He was about thirty years old. His face was like anybody's face.

'One of the waiters said that one night there was a big party and lots of people took photographs,' said Jenny. 'One of the photographers was a friend of one the waiters.'

'That's not a face that people remember,' said Susan. 'But we can use this photograph. We can show the photograph on "Crimeseek". And I would like you to go on "Crimeseek" yourself, Jenny.'

'Me!' said Jenny. 'I can't go on television.'

'Why not?' said Susan. 'Go on the programme. Show people the picture. Tell them what happened. Ask them if they know John Roberts. You'll be fine. And you're very pretty, you know.' Jenny laughed.

'OK, Susan,' said Jenny. 'Thank you. But you're right about John Roberts. He looks like anyone. He doesn't look dangerous, but he is. He's very dangerous.'

'I hope we can help you find John Roberts,' said Susan. 'He's out there, somewhere. Someone knows him.'

'Yes,' said Jenny. 'But we must find him before he finds someone else. We must find him before another person dies.'

Chapter 4   *Waiting*

There's no-one in this street. Only me. No-one can see me. I'm waiting.

Yesterday, at the hospital they said, 'You are well now, John. We need the bed for someone who is ill.' They gave me the name of a house. 'Go to this house,' they said. But I wanted to come here. This is the street where the nurse lives. Nurse Angela.

I followed her yesterday. I followed her home. She lives with another nurse. The nurse is at the hospital in the evening. I watched the house yesterday. No-one saw me. I was behind a wall. I watched Nurse Angela, but she didn't see me.

I'm waiting for Nurse Angela now. Nurse Angela is going to die today. I wanted a friend, but she didn't want to be my friend. The woman in Birmingham didn't want to be my friend. Nurse Angela smiled at me, but I saw how she looked at the doctor. She liked the doctor very much. She didn't like me ... She watched me. She talked about me to the doctor.

I know what I do is wrong. I do bad things. I don't like what I do ... I'm a bad boy ... I go to new places ... This is a new place and I have a new name here ... People don't like me. They talk about me ... People never like me. People always talk about me.

Doctor Cox knew nothing. Yesterday, he went on holiday. I heard him. He said, 'Bye everybody! I'm going to

York for a week on holiday.' And they all said, 'Have a good holiday, Doctor. Have a nice time.' I didn't say anything. But I was thinking. Doctor Cox said goodbye to me.

'Goodbye, John,' said Doctor Cox. Doctor Cox likes Nurse Angela. He's going to be sorry. He *thinks* he's very intelligent but he doesn't know anything. *I'm* very intelligent.

Nurse Angela smiled at me, but she didn't like me. Doctor Cox didn't like me. He talked about me . . . I know these things.

The first time wasn't easy. I said to myself: John, you're a bad boy. Don't do it. But I did it anyway . . . The next time was easy. Women die very quickly.

Here comes Nurse Angela. She's going to find me here in her road.

'Hello,' I say.

*   *   *

Nurse Angela saw John Doe in the road. She knew something was wrong. His new house was not near her street. Why was he here?

'What are you doing here, John?' asked Angela. She wanted to get inside her house quickly. She wanted a hot bath and a hot drink. She did not want to talk in the road with the man called John Doe.

'Hello,' said John Doe. 'I know you. You're Nurse Angela.' He smiled. 'Where am I?' he asked. 'Is my new house near here?'

'Oh no,' thought Angela. 'He can't remember. I thought he was well now. At the hospital everyone thought he was well.'

'I'm cold,' said John.

Angela took his hand. It was very, very cold.

'You need a hot drink,' she said. 'You're very cold.'

'Yes, please,' said John.

'He must go back to the hospital,' thought Angela. 'But first he needs a cup of hot coffee and something to eat.'

'My house is here,' she said.

'Is it?' asked John.

'Come in,' said Angela. She opened the door. She wanted to help the man. He looked so cold and unhappy.

'You are very nice to me,' said John. He walked inside the house. The house was nice and warm. John smiled.

'I'm very hungry,' said John. He smiled again. He knew he had a nice smile.

'Would you like something to eat?' asked Nurse Angela.

'Thank you,' said John. 'Thank you very much, Nurse Angela.'

Chapter 5   *Goodbye, holiday!*

It was a beautiful morning. 'This is good,' thought Philip Cox. 'I love holidays. I can sleep and eat and do nothing. I can be with my family and go and look at the city of York. The hotel is very nice,' thought Philip.

He sat on the large bed and drank his coffee. He never had breakfast in bed at home. There was too much work. There was a television in the hotel bedroom. 'I can watch television and eat my breakfast in bed,' he thought.

'Is it OK if I turn on the television?' he asked his wife.

'Why not?' she said. 'You're on holiday.'

Philip turned on the television.

'Good morning,' said the woman on the television. 'I'm Susan Peters. With me this morning is Detective Jenny Brown.' Jenny Brown smiled.

'I hope you can help us,' said Detective Jenny Brown on the television. 'Last Friday, here in York, a woman died. Her name was Mary. We know that she had dinner with a man called John Roberts. We want to talk to John Roberts.'

There was now a picture of a man on the television.

'Do you know this man?' asked Detective Jenny Brown. 'Is John Roberts his name? Does he have another name? Please, please phone this number if you know him.'

'Oh, no,' said Philip Cox to his wife. 'I know that man. He's in the hospital back in Exeter. We called him John Doe. Goodbye, holiday!'

Philip phoned the number that was on the television programme. He talked to Detective Jenny Brown.

'My name is Doctor Philip Cox. I'm in York on holiday. The man you called John Roberts is in our hospital in Exeter.'

'Can you come to the police station now?' asked Detective Brown.

'Yes, of course,' said Doctor Cox to the detective. 'I can come now.'

The police station was near the hotel and five minutes later Doctor Philip Cox was in Detective Jenny Brown's office.

'Thank you, Doctor Cox,' said Detective Brown. 'Thank you for coming here. I know you are on holiday.'

'That's OK,' said Doctor Cox.

'I phoned your hospital,' Detective Brown said, 'but the man you call John Doe isn't there. He left yesterday.'

Doctor Cox thought for a moment. 'There's a house we use sometimes for people who don't have homes. Is he there?'

'No,' Detective Brown answered. 'I phoned that house. The hospital told him to go there. But the people at the house say he never came. No one knows where he is.'

'This is bad,' said Doctor Cox.

'Yes, it is,' said Detective Brown. 'John Roberts is a very dangerous man.'

'Do you think he's still in Exeter?' asked Doctor Cox.

'I don't know,' said Detective Brown. 'Does he know anyone else in Exeter? Did he talk to anyone else at the hospital?'

'Nurse Angela,' said Doctor Cox. 'I asked Nurse Angela to talk to John Doe a lot, to ask him questions.'

'Can you speak to her?' asked Detective Brown.

'I can phone the hospital,' said Doctor Cox. He phoned the hospital.

'She's not there,' he told Detective Brown. 'She went home three hours ago.'

'Phone her at home!' said Detective Jenny Brown. 'Quick! Quick! Doctor Cox! Get Angela's home telephone number. Find out where she lives. I'm going to phone the Exeter police.'

Chapter 6 *A cup of coffee*

John stood in the kitchen. 'Angela thinks I went to the shop,' he said to himself. 'But I didn't. I didn't go out. I opened the door and I shut the door. But I didn't go out. I came into the kitchen. And now I'm waiting for her.'

The kitchen was white. There were pictures of flowers on the wall. John did not look at the pictures. He looked at the knives. He liked knives.

The telephone rang. Nurse Angela answered it. John walked out of the kitchen very slowly. He had a knife in his hand.

John heard Angela talking. She was talking on the telephone. He couldn't hear the words. He walked towards her.

'Doctor Cox?' Angela asked. 'Is that you? What do you want? Why are you phoning me at home? Aren't you on holiday?'

'Angela,' asked Doctor Cox, 'are you all right? Do you know where John Doe is?'

'Yes, do you want to speak to him?' asked Angela.

'Is John Doe there?' asked Doctor Cox. 'Oh no,' he thought.

'Yes, he was here,' said Angela. 'He waited for me in the street. We're going to have a hot drink. He went out to get me some milk. What is it?'

'Don't open the door, Angela,' said Doctor Cox. 'John Doe is a very dangerous man. The police in York want him. A woman died here.'

'What?' said Angela. Then she heard a noise in the house. She spoke very quietly to Doctor Cox.

'Doctor Cox,' she said, 'I think John is in the house. I can hear him.'

'The Exeter police know what's happening,' said Doctor Cox. 'They are waiting outside your house now. Can you open the door?'

'I think so,' said Angela. Then she saw John. John was by the door. He had a large knife in his hand. 'Hello, John,' said Angela.

Angela stood up.

'I thought you went to get some milk,' she said.

'I was in the kitchen,' said John. 'Who are you talking to on the telephone?'

'It's Doctor Cox,' said Angela. 'He wants to talk to you.'

'I don't want to talk to him,' said John.

'OK,' said Angela. 'But can I talk to you?'

'Yes, you can talk to me,' said John.

Angela put the phone down slowly.

'What are you doing with that knife?' she asked.

'Nothing,' said John Doe. He lifted the knife and smiled. It wasn't a nice smile.

Angela was afraid, but she did not want John to know that she was afraid.

'Would you like a drink now, John?' said Angela. 'I can make you a nice hot drink.'

'OK,' said John. He was still smiling.

She walked into the kitchen. She made the coffee very slowly. John stood close by her with the knife.

Angela could see the police outside the window. And the police could see them. And the knife. They waited. They didn't want John Doe to use the knife. Angela was very afraid now. It was a big knife.

'Here's your coffee,' she said to John. John walked towards her. 'But there's no milk in it,' said Angela, 'because you didn't buy any milk. So it's very hot!'

Angela was very quick. The hot coffee was in the cup, then, the next moment, it was in John's face. John put his hands to his face. The knife went on the floor. Angela ran to the door and opened it. The police ran in. John was on the floor. Then the police took him away in their car.

Angela sat down. She could not speak. A detective came in.

'You were very good, Angela,' she said. 'The police are taking John Roberts to York police station. And it's goodbye, John Doe.' The detective smiled. 'And there's a Doctor Cox on the telephone. He wants to know if you're OK.'